18

24

32

38

The solo trumpet is urged on through this whole piece and joined four and one half
measures from the end by the second trumpet in unison - a tricky spot to "tune".

Ayre

♩ = 40 ♩♩♩♩ intro.

Moderato

p 2nd trpt

5

Solo

p

mf

p

9

rit. last time only

mf

MMO CD 3805

The two trumpets share the melody in the first part of this piece but, towards the end,
the solo trumpet is "let loose" to climax this beautiful movement.

Canzona per sonare No. 2

Giovanni Gabrieli (1557-1612)

MUSIC FOR
BRASS ENSEMBLE

3805

Two Trumpet Tunes and Ayre

Henry Purcell (1659-1695)

Tune One

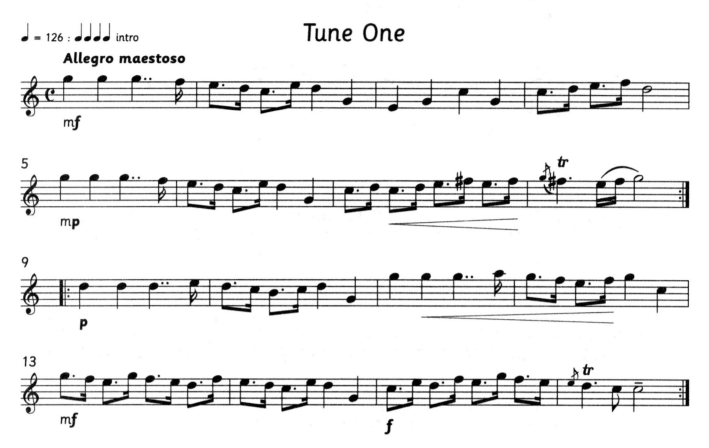

A well-known trumpet solo tastefully arranged by John Corley for brass ensemble. Watch the dynamics and the solo trumpet trills which should start on the beat and from above.

Tune Two

There is a return to the opening section in this exciting piece at D, so help us keep the middle section alive by accenting your three repeated 8th notes starting with letter B.

Three Dances

Tilman Susato (c. 1500- c. 1580)

The Ronde and Saltarelle found here are charming examples of a single melody adapted to two contrasting dance rhythms.

Pavane (Si par souffrir)

♩ = 60 ♩♩♩ intro.

Here is a good test for your breath control.

Sonata No. 19

♩ = 112 ♩♩♩♩ intro.

Gottfried Reiche (1667-1734)

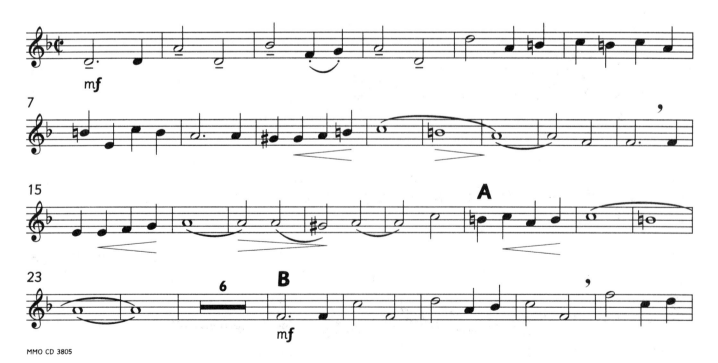

Reiche, the first trumpeter of J. S. Bach, introduced the fugal form for tower music. In this sonata we have a wonderful fugue followed by a recitative-like **Adagio** and a moving **Grave**. The sustained trumpet melody of the **Grave** is echoed in the tuba.

Two pieces

Anthony Holborne (-1602)

Honie-Suckle

Night Watch

Here are two examples of modal harmony full of surprises for our major and minor ears.

Canzona per sonare No. 1 – La Spiritata

Giovanni Gabrieli (1557-1612)

This famous "chain" type canzona has three contrasting sections in style as well as meter.
Hold each note for its full value and play smoothly with a minimum of accents.

Four Pieces

Johann Pezel (1639-1694)

Intrade

The suite, a popular instrumental form during the baroque era, was a group of related pieces in highly stylized dance rhythms. An Intrada usually introduces the suite and in this vigorous one, every part has a thematic entry which should be "hammered" out.

Sarabande

MMO CD 3805

The Sarabande started life as a wild and primitive dance of the American Indian. However, one hundred years after it reached Europe, via the Spanish conquerors, it had become a stately court dance. In this stirring Sarabande, the B♭ major scale of the tuba holds the work together. Homophonic (chordal) passages such as this one call for careful blending with no one of the parts sticking out.

Bal

The two sections of this "ballet-like" piece are played slightly faster when repeated. This, in the style of the time, adds some variation to the performance. Watch the last two measures, they crescendo (grow louder) but the antiphonal bell-tones between the upper voices should not be hidden.

Gigue

MMO CD 3805

The Gigue was traditionally used to bring a suite to a close. Notice how Pezel uses the first subject, only turned upside-down (inverted), for the second section. Once again the thematic entries are hammered out by all the players who then immediately recede into the background.

Sonata No. 22

Johann Pezel (1639-1694)

MMO CD 3805 The trumpets are pitted against the lower voices throughout this typical tower sonata.
Play with partner or partners in mind, matching their articulations and dynamics.

Two pieces

Johann Hermann Schein (1586-1630)

Paduana

This piece, another typical suite movement, is kept alive by the subtle moving voices scattered among all the parts. A delicate balance is found here between a homophonic (chordal) and polyphonic (independent voice lines) style.

Gaillard

The Italian word "gagliarda" means romping and rollicking. Play accordingly.

Sonata No. 2

Johann Pezel (1639-1694)

MMO CD 3805

This sonata is full of echoes, an important feature of baroque music. The last sections begins with a chordal cadence, again echoed, followed by a graceful polyphonic section.

MMO CD 3805
MMO Cass. 6001

Music Minus One

MUSIC FOR BRASS ENSEMBLE
TRUMPET

Band No. Complete Version		Band No. Minus Trumpet	Page No.
1	*Purcell:* Tune 1	21	2
2	Tune 2	22	2
3	Ayre	23	3
4	*Gabrieli:* Canzona No. 2	24	4
5	*Susato:* 3 Dance - Ronde	25	5
6	Salterelle	26	5
7	Pavane	27	6
8	*Reiche:* Sonata No. 19	28	6
9	*Holborne:* Honie-Suckle	29	8
10	Night Watch	30	8
11	*Gabrieli:* Canzona No. 1	31	9
12	*Pezel:* Intrade	32	10
13	Sarabande	33	10
14	Bal	34	11
15	Gigue	35	11
16	*Pezel:* Sonata No. 22	36	12
17	*Schein:* Paduana	37	13
18	Gaillard	38	13
19	*Pezel:* Sonata No. 2	39	14
20	Concert Bb Chord & Tuning Note		

MUSIC MINUS ONE • 50 Executive Boulevard • Elmsford, New York 10523-1325